La Fontaine's Fables

First published in Great Britain 1984 by
André Deutsch Limited
105 Great Russell Street, London WC1

English versions Copyright © 1984 by Diana Athill
Illustrations Copyright © Gautier-Languereau 1982

ISBN 0 233 97713 9

BRITISH LIBRARY CATALOGUING IN PUBLICATION DATA
La Fontaine, Jean de
  La Fontaine's fabels.
  I. Title   II Athill, Diana   III. Fables
de la Fontaine. *English*
  841'.4   PQ1811.E3
                    © Gautier-Languereau 1982
  ISBN 0–233–97713–9 ISBN - 2.217.42000.3

La Fontaine's Fables

English version by Diana Athill

Illustrations by Romain Simon

André Deutsch

Contents

THE GRASSHOPPER AND THE ANT

The Grasshopper, all summer long,
chirruped song after song.
When winter winds began to roar
she found herself poor.
No scrap of worm, no wing of fly
had she put by.

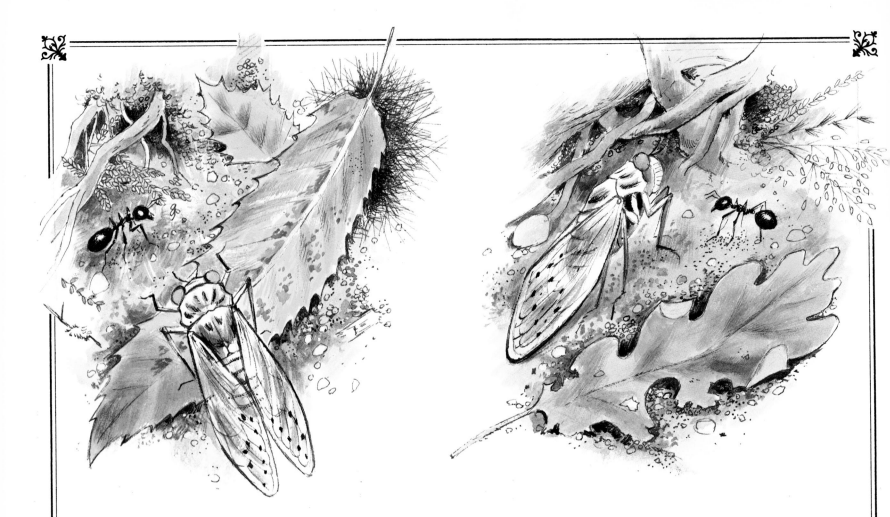

She had no choice, a-begging she went
to her neighbour the Ant.
"I have nothing left to eat!
Lend me some wheat.

I'll repay you, never fear,
I promise and swear,
plus an ounce for every pound
you lend me, my dear."

The Ant, though willing to befriend her,
was not a lender.
"What, good neighbour, let me ask,
was your summer task?"
"Day and night, all summer long,
I sang song after song."

"You *sang* all summer? How entrancing!
You'd better spend the winter dancing."

THE CROW AND THE FOX

Mr Crow, perched in a tree,
held a cheese for the Fox to see.
Mr Fox, with a wicked leer,
spoke these words for the Crow to hear.

"Oh how handsome! Upon my word
I've never seen a more glamorous bird.
What a shame that your ugly croak
turns your beauty to a joke."

"It's *not* a croak," croaked Mr Crow,
letting – of course – his camembert go.
"Thanks!" said Fox as he picked it up.
"Observe that flatterers always sup
at the expense of vanity –
a lesson you can't expect for free."
"I'll never be caught again that way,"
swore angry Crow – a bit late in the day,
wouldn't you say?

THE FROG WHO LONGED TO BE AS
BIG AS AN OX

A silly little frog
a stately Bullock spies,
and, smitten with his size,
longs to be as big.
She sucks in air. With every huff and puff
she cries, "Watch me! Am I yet big enough?"
– "Noo," moos the Ox – "Well, now?" – "Noo noo," again,
but still the Frog goes on to puff and strain.
"You're noowhere near it, you had better stop."
But Froggie doesn't listen – and goes POP.

The world is full of sillies
puffing up their bellies.
They only have to see
a bigger man to be
afflicted with the swellies.

THE WOLF AND THE DOG

A Wolf, all bones beneath his ragged skin
(because fierce dogs guarded the flocks so well)
once met a mastiff very far from thin,
sleek, smug and handsome, sound as any bell.
    Oh, how Wolf longed to slice him up
    and on his tender flesh to sup!
But he could see this was no easy dinner –
come to a fight, and Dog would be the winner.
    Better to humbly greet
    this toothsome chunk of meat
and compliment him on his prosperous state.

"It's up to you, dear sir," the Dog replied,
"to be as plump as me. Within these woods
I see that everyone is lean and gaunt,
and so would I be, if I had relied –
as you do – on my fangs to win me goods
    and rescue me from want.
    Come home with me, and share
    my princely fare."

"What would I have to do," said Wolf, "to earn it?"
    "Little, and you'd soon learn it.
Chase off a beggar or two, fawn on a friend,
flatter your master; and there'd be no end
to rich, delicious dinners – not forgetting
plenty of very gratifying petting."
    Weeping for joy, the Wolf agreed
    to go with him. But as they sped
    along the path he suddenly saw
    a nasty spot, all red and raw,
    on the Dog's neck. "What's that?" he cried.
    "Nothing at all," the Dog replied.
"It can't be nothing," said the Wolf. "You're bleeding."
"Perhaps my collar chafed me." – "Aren't you free
to run where you wish, when you have done with feeding?"
"Sometimes I'm not – but what's so bad about it?"
"Your liberty – you have to do without it!"
    "So what? It doesn't worry me."
"If *that* doesn't worry you, nothing ever will."
And away ran Wolf. They say he's running still.

THE TOWN MOUSE AND THE COUNTRY MOUSE

A Town Mouse, once upon a time,
asked a Country Mouse to dinner,
most politely offering
a feast that wouldn't leave them thinner.

Every kind of food was scattered
on the carpet. Need I say
that the friends tucked into it
with relish and without delay.

Such smells! Such flavours! What a treat!
The entertainment was perfection . . .
till suddenly – oh dear oh dear –
a most alarming interjection!

A sound – a most purrturrbing sound.
Someone – or something? – at the door!
Host and guest, quick as a flash,
scuttled off across the floor.

Silence again. It's gone away?
"Come," said the host, "let's not be beaten.
There's plenty left, we'll not give up
until the lot is eaten."

"Thank you, but no," said Country Mouse.
"Tomorrow you must come to me.
My food is not as good as yours
but my dining-room is free
from interrupting Things. I eat
entirely at my leisure,
and much prefer a calm, plain meal
to your nerve-racking pleasure."

THE WOLF AND THE LAMB

Might is right: if you don't know it
allow me with this tale to show it.

At a sparkling stream
a little Lamb was drinking.
Out of the shadowy wood
a Wolf came slinking.
"Lamb," snarled the Wolf, "You're mucking up my water,
so I intend to lead you to the slaughter."

"My Lord – Your Majesty," stammered the Lamb,
"kindly observe that as I sip I am
downstream – a long way down, I truly think,
from that transparent pool where you will drink."

"You've mucked it up.
And what is more, I know
that just a year ago
you called me an idle, cheeky, thieving pup."

"A year ago, my Lord, I wasn't born . . .
Oh please, I beg of you, ask my woolly mother!"
– "Well, if it wasn't you it must have been
that foul-mouthed reprobate your elder brother."
– "I have no brother!" – "So – who cares? It was
someone to do with you: a close relation –
your shepherd – his dog – your who-knows-what. And I
must now avenge my damaged reputation.

Whereupon – snap, gobble, crunch,
he ate the Lamb for lunch.

THE FOX AND THE STORK

When Mrs Stork accepted Mr Fox's invitation
she soon became quite furious – nay, bilious – with frustration.
A wishy-washy soup was all he served; and worse than that:
it came in shallow dishes which were very nearly flat.
Imagine, if you will, a stork trying to eat
with her long pointed bill from a flat, shallow plate.
"Dear me," said Mr Fox, "we mustn't let it go to waste."
And he lapped up every drop of it before she'd had a taste.

So

When Mrs Stork invited Mr Fox to come to dinner
she served a most delicious meal – it really was a winner.
Mr Fox felt almost faint on sniffing the first course –
the meat was bathed in such a fragrant, such a tempting sauce.
But . . . it was served in vases with tall, narrow necks
which might have been designed and made especially to vex
an animal who hadn't got a long, pointed bill
and had to use a shallow dish if he would eat his fill.
A fox outwitted by a bird! It was too much to bear.
With his tail between his legs he hurried homewards to his lair.

I tell this tale for tricksters: I would like to see them learn
that those who cheat their neighbours, get cheated in return.

THE OAK TREE AND THE REED

    Said the Oak Tree to the Reed:
    "Your lot is hard, indeed.
To one so slim and frail a mere goldcrest
seems like a burden, and you're forced to bend
by the softest airs. While I, my little friend,
am weather-proof, and never fail the test
or raging storms. Your hurricane's my breeze.

You could, of course, enjoy a life of ease
    if you could grow
      just here, below
my canopy, and not beside the lake –
a windy spot! I worry for your sake."
"Your worry does you credit," said the Reed,
"proving your heart is kind. But there's no need,
    compassionate Tree,
      to waste anxiety on me.
Better than you the boisterous winds I take:
    I bend, I do not break.
So far, I know, tempest and hurricane
have thumped your gallant sturdiness in vain,
    but I foresee, with pain . . ."

Even as she spoke, a gale came thundering forth
out of the fearsome cauldron of the north.
    The Reed most gracefully gave way.
    The mighty Oak refused to sway.
    The Reed survived. The tree, whose head
reached for the sky, while his roots found
their hold among the buried dead,
measured his length along the ground.

THE LION AND THE MOUSE

Let us always keep in mind
that it pays us to be kind.
Even a grateful Mouse
can sometimes be of use.

A careless one once ran between a Lion's paws.
The gracious king of beasts didn't crunch him in his jaws
but granted him his life, not dreaming of reward,
for what could Mousie ever do for such a mighty Lord?

Well, there came a dreadful day when Lion, at a bend
in a pathway through the forest very nearly met his end.
He was trapped in a hunter's net, stretched between tree and tree,
and with all his rage and muscle was unable to break free.

Hearing the Lion's roar the little Mouse came scurrying,
and nibble, nibble, nibble – carefully, not hurrying,
he gnawed right through the rope so the net fell into bits.
It wasn't power that did the trick, but patience and sharp wits.

THE PIGEON AND THE ANT

A similar lesson can be learnt
from the Pigeon and the Ant.

The Ant fell into a stream and nearly sank.
The kindly Pigeon threw her a blade of grass
round which her waving pincers she could pass –
the Ant caught hold, and safely reached the bank.

Soon afterwards a horrid boy came by
        armed with a bow and arrow.
"That pigeon," he thought, "is just the thing for my
        supper tomorrow."
He drew his bow – then gave a piercing squeal:
the grateful Ant had bitten his naked heel.
        Alerted by his cry
        away the bird did fly –
        and so did pigeon pie.

THE HARE AND THE FROGS

A Hare in his form was lying low
and brooding (there's little else to do
when lying low) on his hard lot
in living a life of fear and fret.
"How wretchedly our natures serve us –
those of us created nervous.
Just look at me: my sleepless nights,
ruined digestion, frantic flights!
'Pull yourself together' they say,
        but when did fear
        such counsel hear?
I only wish I *could* obey."

Suddenly his twitching ears
picked up a harmless sound. His fears
turned it sinister. Off he sped,
fleeing his warm, unthreatened bed,
desperate for a safer shelter.
He passed a pond – when helter-skelter,
plip, plop, plip, frogs by the score
leapt terrified into the water.
"Goodness gracious!" said the Hare.
"Those timid creatures take me for
a very thunderbolt of war.
I frighten them – can such things be? –
as other people frighten me!"
It seems that a coward can always find
even worse cowards to ease his mind.

THE COCK AND THE FOX

High in a tree there sat a wise old Cock
keeping a canny eye on all who passed.
A Fox called up to him: "Friend, good news at last!
Peace reigns between us foxes and your flock.
Come down, and let me kiss you as a brother –
    hurry, for I must run
to carry the happy message to the other
members of the farmyard. You and they
can celebrate tonight. Bonfires and fun
can mark your safety from us beasts of prey.
But meanwhile let me clasp you in my paws
    in honour of this historic day
    when our traditional coldness thaws."

"Oh Fox," said the Cock, "never has news been heard
sweeter to beast and bird.
And doubly I rejoice
to hear it from your voice.
Yonder I see a couple of hounds careering
in our direction. They, too, must be bearing
this news. They're almost here. I will come down
to share with all three of you the brotherly kiss . . .
But friend, why do you frown?"
Said the flustered Fox: "I'll have to give it a miss –
so busy – another time – don't think me rude . . ."
And off ran Fox as fast as ever he could
to hide his disappointment in the wood.

How the Cock chuckled! A trick seems twice as neat
if the person cheated is himself a cheat.

THE WOLF TURNED SHEPHERD

A Wolf who'd been going short of mutton
thought he might remedy this fact
by learning how to act.
He put a shepherd's cloak and hat on,
stole some bagpipes, found a stick
that looked like a shepherds's crook,
and said: "We all know sheep are silly.
When I appear in this disguise
before their undiscerning eyes
they'll take me for their shepherd, Willie."

On his hind legs, propped by his crook,
false Willie tiptoed round the flock.
Meanwhile real Willie, with his dog
lay in the grass and slept like a log.
To drive the sheep to his own estate
false Willie had to imitate
real Willie's voice – and thought he could.
But when he gave his shepherd's call
the sound which echoed through the wood
was not like Willie's voice at all.
It certainly woke the sheep; moreover
it woke the shepherd and good dog Rover.
For poor old Wolf this was no joke.
His legs got tangled in his cloak,
he could neither fight nor run away –
What happened to him I needn't say.

Some little detail always catches out
those who pretend to be what they are not.

THE FOX AND THE BILLY GOAT

A swaggering Fox, unscrupulous and sly,
went walking with a Goat of simple mind.
The day was hot, and soon their throats were dry.
The only water that the Fox could find –
using his highly developed sense of smell –
lay at the very bottom of a well.

They clambered down and freely quenched their thirst.
Said Fox: "Having drunk until we nearly burst,
we've got to think how to get out of here.
　　Suppose you rear
and play the ladder up against the wall,
stretching as high as you can; then, in no time,
on to your back, and up, and out I'll climb,
and pull you after. Come now, make yourself tall."

　　The Goat agreed.
　　"Dear Fox," he said,
"having you here is most tremendous luck.
Left to myself I'm sure I'd be quite stuck."

So up skipped Fox. But did he help the Goat
to follow him? Indeed he didn't. Instead,
　"You silly Billy," he said,
"before going down that well you should have thought.
And now I've got a thousands things to do
so I must fly – can't possibly wait for you.
　Get out as best you may."
　And Fox went on his way.

Whatever your undertaking, think it through.

THE WOLF AND THE STORK

It is wolfish nature to eat greedily,
    and one of them, a typical glutton,
    gobbled up a leg of mutton
so fast that he choked. It seemed that speedily
his end would come, because the bone had stuck
deep in his throat. By chance a passing Stork
noticed Wolf's gurgling (he could not longer speak)
    and saw that he was choking.
So, with her sensitive and probing beak
she fished out the bone. The surgery over, she
politely asked him for a modest fee.
"A fee?" her patient said. "You must be joking!
    You would now be dead
if I had not refrained from biting off your head.
    Have you no gratitude?
Take care that never again do I have to see
a bird with such a shameless attitude."

THE FOX AND THE GRAPES

A starving Fox was eagerly designing
to steal a bunch of grapes; but try as he might,
he couldn't jump or scramble to their height.
He'd had no breakfast, lunch or tea, and now there'd be no dining.

"So who wants grapes!" said he. "I'm not repining.
They're sour and disgusting. Let the birds
finish them off." And these defiant words
were better, in my opinion, then snivelling and whining.

THE DONKEY AND THE LAP-DOG

There's never any point
in forcing out of joint
your natural gifts, if any.
It isn't given to many
to have outstanding charm.
Settle for what you are
– you may not travel far
but you will not come to harm.

A Donkey wondered: "Why does Master dote
on that silly little dog, while whacks and toil
   are all I get?
It can't be just his size and his woolly coat
which make the family so unfairly spoil
   their favourite pet.

What does he *do* for it? Their hands he licks,
and he jumps on their laps, which makes them kiss and praise.
    Now, I could learn those tricks
and imitate his simpering little ways."
So, lashing his tail, he lifts his horny hoof
and strokes – or rather bruises – his master's face,
    meanwhile raising the roof
    with loving but raucous brays.

"Good lord!" yells Master, "Donkey's gone quite mad!
Quickly, my stick!" – and he thumps him with such rage
    that poor old Donkey's glad
to gallop as fast as he can right off this page.

THE JAY IN THE FEATHERS OF A PEACOCK

A moulting peacock's feathers, once, were stolen
by a Jay who stuck them in among his own
and then, with foolish vanity quite swollen,
went off to strut his beauty on the lawn.
None of the other peacocks were deceived.
They jostled and whistled and jeered, and soon the Jay
lost all his borrowed plumage and, bereaved,
flew home – but even there was turned away.
There are jays in plenty, looking like you and me,
who deck themselves in other people's plumes.
"Copycats" is the word by which they're known,
and I could name you several, but will be
discreet. I don't believe in causing glooms.
I'll leave their business to them, and mind my own.

44

THE WOLF,
THE NANNY GOAT AND THE KID

Needing fresh grass, the Goat went out,
but first the stable door she shut
and locked. She told her Kid: "Now, mind –
the watchword's 'Down with Wolf and all his kind'.
    So promise me:
without those words you do not turn the key
    or even touch the latch."
A lurking Wolf who was keeping hungry watch
    was tickled pink these words to catch.

As soon as the careful Goat was out of sight
　　　the wolf emerged in high delight
　　　to exploit his lucky find.
"Down with the Wolf," he said, "and all his kind –
　　　now let me in, my dear.
　　　You have no need to fear."
But the Kid – no sucker – bleated "Show a paw!
If it isn't white you'll not get through this door . . ."
　　　and as you know,
a wolf's unlikely to have feet of snow.
This one, flummoxed, knew not what to say.
Hungry he'd come, and hungry he went away.

　　　Where would the Kid have been
　　　if he'd trusted only one
　　　safety measure? Caution
　　　can't be overdone.

THE TWO POTS

"Let's take a walk," said the Iron Pot,
but the Earthenware had rather not.
    He thought the kitchen hearth
    the safest place on earth
    for one so very brittle.
    "It takes," he said, "so little
    to crack, or even break, me.
    Don't attept to make me
    venture out. But you yourself
    need not stay upon the shelf."
    To which the Iron Pot replied:
    "But I'd be at your side –
    I'd be your bodyguard
    against anything that's hard.
Any blow which happened to come our way
I would deflect. So come now – what do you say?"

    The Earthen Pot, thus coddled,
    agreed to venture out.
    Both were three-legged and stout
    and rather bad at walking.
    As side by side they waddled,
    deeply engaged in talking,
    they kept bumping one another.
    It hurt the Earthen brother,
    but before he could complain –
    wobble and bump again
    and he lay in little bits.

    Choose company that fits
    your nature, or you'll be
    as broken up as he.

THE BEAR AND THE TWO FRIENDS

Two friends in need of cash, and bold,
a bearskin to a furrier sold
    although the bear still wore it.
They'd kill him soon, or so they said,
and when that king of bears was dead
    the furrier – they swore it –
could make of his luxurious pelt
at least two coats. No one who dealt
in skins, they promised, had seen a better.
The furrier would be their debtor
however much he paid. The skin
in two days' time they would bring in.

So off they went, and found the bear . . .
and courage melted into air.
So huge and threatening was he
that one of them bolted up a tree
while t'other fell flat and hoped to be
mistaken for a corpse (it's said
that bears don't prey upon the dead).
He lay stone still and held his breath.
The foolish bear poked with his nose
and thought: "This isn't a mere pose.
The creature stinks. Yes, this is death," –
and went away. The man in the tree
descended cautiously to see
his comrade lying in the dirt
but happily more scared than hurt.

"What did he say, that mighty bear,
when he was whispering in your ear?"

"He gave this warning: Never dare
again to sell the skin of a bear
which its owner hasn't ceased to wear."

THE LITTLE MOUSE, THE COCK AND THE CAT

This is the story of an infant mouse
whose inexperience proved nearly fatal.
One day he came panting back to his mother's house,
saying: "Mother, I travelled so far! Now just you wait till
I tell you what – beyond the hills – I found:
    Two most amazing creatures!
One of them was gracious, gentle and kind,
the other violent, with alarming features.
    His voice was loud and rude
    and something raw and red
    he wore upon his head.
His arms – if arms they were – he waved like mad,
and his enormous tail was multi-hued."
(The exotic beast which had given him such a shock
    was – you've guessed – a cock.)
"He made such terrifying song and dance
that, brave though I am (as you, I know, agree)
    I had to flee . . .

And wasn't I furious! For it spoilt my chance
of speaking to the other one – the sweet
velvetty one, so full of modest grace
    whom I so longed to meet.
She had a winning expression on her face.
    Her eyes were soft and bright,
    her colour subtle – I'm quite
sure, from her fur, which is short and dense and grey
that she's related to us in some way.
I was going to greet her, when the violent one
made the fearful noise from which I had to run."

"My child," said his mother, "that sweet thing was a cat,
    a dreadful hypocrite,
the sworn enemy of mouse and rat.

The noisy animal, you'll find,
    is useful to our kind –
we sometimes even eat him; but the puss
    eats us.
From this day forth I hope you will believe
that appearances can easily deceive."

THE STAG SEEING HIMSELF
IN THE WATER

A Stag, one day, admiring
his antler's image in a spring,
was seriously disappointed
to see his legs so thin and knobby-jointed.

"I see – and the knowledge gives me pain –
that I'm partly handsome, partly plain.
Compared with my antlers and my face
my spindle-shanks are simply a disgrace."

53

An interruption makes him freeze:
a stag-hound baying! Thoroughly shaken,
into the sheltering forest he flees,
plunging his way through briar and bracken.
But he's trapped by branches as they catch
in his spiky crown: it certainly does not match
his legs, because it hinders him, while they,
given a chance, would speed him on his way.

Let him remind us that we all incline
to despise the useful and admire the fine:
a foolish preference: ornament's worth less,
at many times, then good plain usefulness.

THE TORTOISE AND THE HARE

Speed isn't everything; how you start is more
important: witness the Tortoise and the Hare.
"I'll beat you to that tree-stump," Tortoise said.
"Beat me, Grannie? You really must be mad!
    You need a doctor's care."
    – "Do I? Well, mad or not
    I will stand by my bet."
    So a prize was fixed on (what
    it was I quite forget)
and Hare, so practised at escaping hounds,
knew he could win it in half a dozen bounds.

He had time to browse,
he had time to nap,
he had time to sniff the wind and lap
the dew; while Tortoise, in her house,
set off at a laborious trudge,
as ponderous as any judge.

The Hare felt it would be disgrace
to *try* to win this easy race.
Give her a start and take it easy,
win it casually, like a tease. He
saw his strategy plain as day
and several minutes he spent in play . . .
Then suddenly noticed she was almost there.
Whoops! He must run – and so he did. Too late!
She reached the tree-stump first. "You silly Hare!
You really think I need a doctor's care?
Of course you can run at a much faster rate,
but still I beat you, though my pace is slow
and I have to carry my house wherever I go."

THE ANIMALS STRICKEN WITH THE PLAGUE

Heaven was angry at the crimes
committed by earthlings: fearful times
followed, when everyone was ill.
It was the dreaded plague, which spread
among the animals until
all sickened, and would soon be dead.
The wolves and foxes stalked no more.
Against their prey they raised no paw
        for appetite had fled.
The turtle-doves no longer cooed
but huddled lonely in the wood
        and no more love was made.

The Lion called a meeting. "My dear friends,
we have sinned. We are being punished. To make amends
we must ask the guiltiest animal to give
his life as a sacrifice for the common weal.
Heaven might then consent the rest to heal
and in exchange for one, many might live.

It has been done before when the gods have frowned,
    so friends, I now appeal:
    speak out, nothing conceal
of what, on examining conscience, you have found.
I will begin. Sheep-killing is my crime –
and had the poor creatures harmed me? Not at all.
Moreover it has happened from time to time
that I've munched up a shepherd lad as well.
I'm willing to be sacrificed for our nation,
but think it only fair that all should try
to make an honest, public declaration
so that the very worst of us shall die."

"Sir Lion," said the Fox, "you are too good.
You blame yourself for nothing. What is wrong
with using idiotic sheep as food?
　　Eating the woolly throng,
　　you honour them. As for the lad,
for such as he, nothing can be too bad.
Is he not one of those who think they rule us
and always do everything they can to fool us?"
　　Thus spoke the Fox to loud applause,
and all the other beasts who inspire fear,
　　such as the Tiger and the Bear,
　　with their long teeth and jagged claws,
had their worst sins dismissed as slight or quaint
and each was told he almost was a saint.

Then came the Donkey's turn: "Alas!
Once, in the Abbott's field (I fear it
must have been some evil spirit
tempting me) I ate some grass –
quite a big tuft – and had no right
to taste the very smallest bite."
Oh, what an uproar at these words
as the indignant beasts and birds
led by a righteous wolf, all cursed
the ass: he was by far the worst
sinner among them. He – said they –
had caused the plague, so he must pay.
How *could* he have done such a thing?
No doubt about it, he must swing.

A court can always see at once
who is weak and who is strong,
and that it is which will decide
whether you are right or wrong.

THE HERON
AND THE SNAIL

With his lanky legs and his snaky neck
a thoughtful Heron stood
upon the bank of a little brook
that was full of heron-food.
A succulent carp came swimming by
conversing with a pike.
Now that is just the dish, thought I,
that herons really like.
But not at all. His appetite
was not – or so he felt – quite right.

A fussy bird, he always frowns
on eating random snacks;
but later, when time for dinner comes,
a proper meal he lacks.
The only fish he sees approach
is a skinny, bony little roach –
not nearly good enough.
"I never touch such stuff.
What – me, a heron, eat such humble fare!
What, may I ask, do you take me for, dear sir?
I'll wait for something better." But
next came a minnow, which was not!

    Finally his desperate need
    forced him to assail
    and eat with quite unseemly greed
    a miserable snail.

Always picking, always chosing –
that will often end in losing.

THE MILKMAID AND THE POT OF MILK

Perrette, with a pot of milk upon her head,
    was on her way to town.
Wearing flat heels and a short-skirted gown,
she swung along with a light and easy tread.

She thought: "When my milk is sold
I'll have a coin of gold.
A hundred eggs I'll buy.
Three sittings they will make,
and when they hatch – then I
into the yard will take
the chicks, and rear them well.
My profit, when I sell,
will bring me in a pig.
I'll fatten him easily, and when he's big
he'll make me serious money. Am I absurd
if I think of a cow with a calf at heel? Why not!

Oh, I can see them frisking with the herd . . ."
and she gave a little skip. Off flew the pot
    and all the milk was spilt.
Goodbye, goodbye to calf, cow, pig and eggs.
The woman of property, kicking up her legs
    lost everything but guilt.
Home she went, and I'm sorry to say one fears
that her angry husband was going to box her ears.

Don't count your chickens before they hatch, they say:
wisdom which came into being on that day.

THE WEASEL AND THE RABBIT

The cunning Weasel, one fine day,
stole the house of Johnnie Rabbit.
Johnnie'd gone out, as was his habit,
to eat his breakfast, frisk and play
and dance his early morning dance.
"Aha!" said Weasel. "He's away!" –
and seized her chance.

Johnnie came home and found her there.
"Heavens!" he cried. "What do I see!
This residence belongs to me
and was my father's long before.
I'll set the rats on you, you bold
and greedy thing." Said Weasel: "Here
I am, and here I stay. I'm told
that to have is, legally, to hold.

I'd like to know what power ordains
that homes for ever and a day
within one family should stay?"
– "But it's by *law* that it remains
with me," said Johnnie. "Lawyers know it,
and with their help I'll make you pay.
I'm in the right, and they will show it."

"Perhaps," said Weasel, "we had better go
and ask Grimalkin. He is sure to know."
Grimalkin was a famous hermit cat,
grave in his manner, fluffy and very fat.
He was reputed infinitely wise.
"Yes," said Johnnie. "Let's see what he'll advise."

Grimalkin said: "Come near, my chucks, come near.
I'm old, and find it difficult to hear.
Closer. Come close." And when they were in reach,
with a lightning left and right he caught them each
a fearful blow, their argument to conclude
by turning them both into Grimalkin food.

It was like the past, when petty lords would bring
their tiffs to be decided by a king.
Could similar incidents occur today?
    I wouldn't like to say.

THE TWO RATS AND THE EGG

Two Rats are foraging, and find an egg:
dinner for both – they do not need a leg
of mutton or a brisket. Full of glee
    they settle down to eat it.
    But wait! What do they see?
Here's Mr Fox approaching. They must beat it
and save their egg. But how? You cannot drag
something you cannot grasp. It is too big
    for any rat to hold,
    too fragile to be rolled,
and they haven't time to make a carrier-bag.

Necessity to invention gives an edge:
one of them lies on his back – becomes a sledge!
He clutches the egg to his belly, while the other –
bumpety bump – tows home his supine brother,
using his tail as rope. After which, never
presume to say that animals aren't clever.

THE TORTOISE AND THE TWO DUCKS

A restless Tortoise, tired of her hovel,
conceived a passionate desire to travel
(for foreign parts are often over-rated,
and homely comforts are by cripples hated).
Two Ducks, to whom she told
her project bold
declared they could provide the means whereby
she might her eager longing satisfy.
"Our boundless realm," they said, "the upper air,
is yours to command, for we know how to bear
you far away. Such kingdoms you will see!
So many customs learn! Your mind will be
broadened past recognition."

Pleased by their proposition,
Tortoise cried "Done!" This was the Ducks' invention:
they'd carry a stick, which she her jaws would clench on.
"Now hang on tight," they said, "and don't let go," –
    then seized the stick at either end
    and whisked their shell-encumbered friend,
to everyone's amazement, up in the air.
    It was a splendid show –
no wonder everybody stopped to stare.

"A miracle!" they cried. "Look up in the sky –
there goes the Queen of the Tortoises gliding by!"

"The Queen? Why yes – that's just what I must be."
said Tortoise – only to wish at once that she
had kept her mouth shut. Down, down, down she fell,
and shattered into smithereens her shell.

Imprudence, foolish vanity,
and idle curiosity
go hand in hand, to ill effect,
exactly as you would expect.

THE WOLF AND THE FOX

Now why does Aesop claim that foxes are
the cleverest? Wolf has a mind that is faster
when saving his skin – or slitting that of another.
He's quite as cunning as his small red brother.
I hesitate to argue with my master,
but think I could prove the Wolf to be the star.
    Yet here's a tale which *does* imply
    that Fox excels at being sly.

One night he saw the moon reflected deep
in the bottom of a well, and took it for
a cheese, so white and round. They used to keep
two buckets at a well-head: one would soar
as the other plunged – and Fox went down in one,
only to see that he had been mistaken
    and to feel very shaken
    because it was quite plain
    he couldn't get up again.

The only way, he saw, it could be done
was if some other hungry or greedy one
should, seeing the same imaginary cheese,
descend in the other bucket, and raise his.

Two days elapsed, and nobody came by,
while passing time, as usual, took a bite
out of the moon's full circle. On the third night
behold the Wolf – and hungry. Fox called: "Hi!
Brother! I've got a treat for you. Look here –
 See this not quite perfect sphere?
 It's a cheese so heavenly that I
 could not resist a nibble; but
 I've kept the best of it for you.
 Hop in that bucket. Come and put
 it to the test. You'll find it true
that it's divine." The silly Wolf was fooled.
He quickly descended, and as quickly pulled
Fox out of trouble. But don't mock him. We
 are often no less daft than he.
 The greedy are quite easy to deceive
 because they are so anxious to believe.

Achevé d'imprimer sur les presses
en l'Imprimerie Lazare-Ferry à Paris
Dépôt légal : juillet 1984 - N° d'Éditeur 5083